AUSTRALIA

By Jennifer Lombardo
and Alicia Z. Klepeis

EXPLORING WORLD CULTURES

Cavendish Square

Published in 2024 by Cavendish Square Publishing, LLC
2544 Clinton Street, Buffalo, NY 14224

Second Edition

Website: cavendishsq.com

Library of Congress Cataloging-in-Publication Data
Names: Lombardo, Jennifer, author. | Klepeis, Alicia, 1971- author.
Title: Australia / Jennifer Lombardo and Alicia Z. Klepeis.
Description: Second edition. | Buffalo, NY : Cavendish Square Publishing, [2024] | Series: Exploring world cultures | Includes bibliographical references and index.
Identifiers: LCCN 2023028314 | ISBN 9781502670021 (library binding) | ISBN 9781502670014 (paperback) | ISBN 9781502670038 (ebook)
Subjects: LCSH: Australia--Juvenile literature.
Classification: LCC DU96 .K54 2024 | DDC 994--dc23/eng/20230629
LC record available at https://lccn.loc.gov/2023028314

Writers: Alicia Z. Klepeis; Jennifer Lombardo (second edition)
Editor: Jennifer Lombardo
Copyeditor: Danielle Haynes
Designer: Andrea Davison-Bartolotta

The photographs in this book are used by permission and through the courtesy of: Cover Tatiana Gordievskaia/Shutterstock.com; p. 4 Peter Hermes Furian/Shutterstock.com; p. 5 iacomino FRiMAGES/Shutterstock.com; p. 6 Tong Shen/Shutterstock.com; p. 7 coloursinmylife/Shutterstock.com; p. 8 Janelle Lugge/Shutterstock.com; p. 9 File:Neville Bonner 1979.jpg/Wikimedia Commons; p. 10 Leonid Andronov/Shutterstock.com; p. 11 Naga11/Shutterstock.com; pp. 12 (right), 16 Taras Vyshnya/Shutterstock.com; p. 12 (left) Nils Versemann/Shutterstock.com; p. 13 kwest/Shutterstock.com; p. 14 (right) Madelein Wolfaardt/Shutterstock.com; p. 14 (left) TRW Creations/Shutterstock.com; p. 15 Katherine Wallis/Shutterstock.com; p. 17 LittlePanda29/Shutterstock.com; p. 18 fritz16/Shutterstock.com; p. 19 Olga Kashubin/Shutterstock.com; p. 20 myphotobank.com.au/Shutterstock.com; p. 21 NNNMMM/Shutterstock.com; p. 22 Michal Pesata/Shutterstock.com; p. 23 James Davis Photography/Shutterstock.com; p. 24 Sergio Gutierrez Getino/Shutterstock.com; p. 25 katacarix/Shutterstock.com; p. 26 ChameleonsEye/Shutterstock.com; p. 27 Darren Tierney/Shutterstock.com; p. 28 Leonard Zhukovsky/Shutterstock.com; p. 29 Mark Camenzuli/Shutterstock.com.

CPSIA compliance information: Batch #CW24CSQ: For further information contact Cavendish Square Publishing LLC at 1-877-980-4450.

Printed in the United States of America

CONTENTS

INTRODUCTION

The island country of Australia is located in a part of the world called Oceania. The country has a long and rich history. Its people come from all over the world. The country's government is a **democracy**.

People in Australia work many kinds of jobs. Some are farmers or national park rangers. Others are bankers, hotel workers, or teachers. Miners dig in

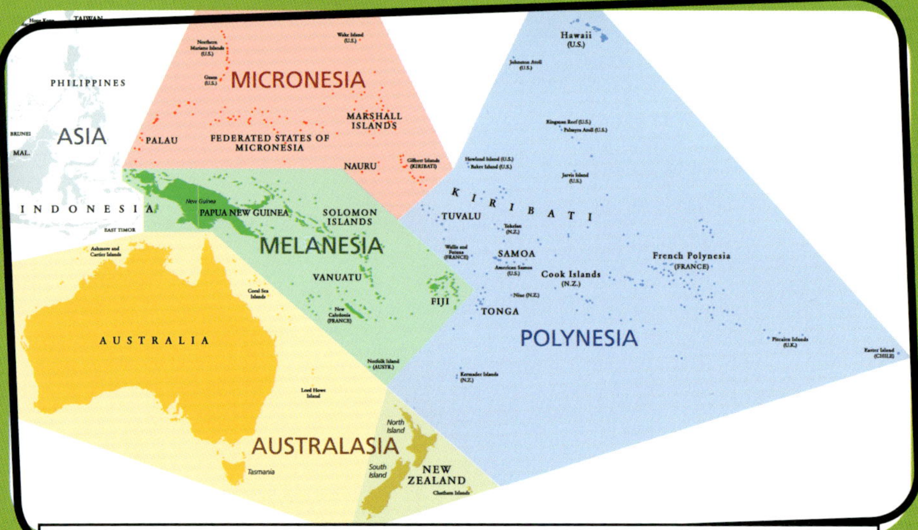

Within Oceania, there are smaller areas that have their own names. This map shows which countries are included in Oceania and the names of the areas.

the ground for gold and other **valuable** items. Some Australians make machines.

Australia has some beautiful places to visit, including deserts, beaches, mountains, and rain forests. It is also known for its large **variety** of animals and plants. Australian families often enjoy camping and spending time in nature, but they need to be careful. Some dangerous, or unsafe, animals in Australia include spiders, jellyfish, and snakes.

Many Australians like to play sports. They also like music, books, and art. There's a lot to love about this country!

In Australia, there are large stretches of empty space called the outback.

GEOGRAPHY

Australia is the smallest **continent** in the world. At 2,969,975 square miles (7,692,199 square kilometers), it's a little smaller than the main part of the United States.

Most of Australia is flat, but the country does have some mountains. The Blue and Snowy Mountains are two examples. The Great Dividing Range stretches for 2,300 miles (3,700 km) through eastern and southeastern Australia.

FACT!

A large rock called Uluru is sacred, or very important, to the Aboriginal people who live near it.

This picture shows part of Blue Mountain National Park.

Because the outback is so empty and dark, it's a great place to stargaze.

More than one-third of Australia is desert. In many parts of the country, it's very hot and water is hard to find. Most people live in southeastern and southwestern Australia, where it's cooler and there's more water.

STATES AND TERRITORIES

Australia is split into six states: New South Wales, Victoria, Queensland, Western Australia, South Australia, and Tasmania. There are also 10 **territories**, including the Northern Territory and the Australian Capital Territory.

HISTORY

The first people to arrive in Australia are known as Aboriginal, or Indigenous, Australians. They came to the country more than 50,000 years ago.

In the early 1600s, Europeans arrived. Beginning in 1788, Britain started sending many of its prisoners to Australia. At first, these Europeans got along with the Aboriginal peoples. Later, they fought over who owned the land. When gold was found, the British started taking Aboriginal land. They made the people move to other parts of Australia.

In the 1840s, Europeans brought camels to Australia to help them travel through the desert. Today, there are many wild camels in the outback.

In 1901, Australia became one country. Its full name is the **Commonwealth** of Australia. During the 20th century, people moved to Australia from all over the world. Today, the Indigenous people still face a lot of **racism** from other Australians, including the government.

FACT!

Another main group of Indigenous Australians are the Torres Strait Islanders. They have their roots in the Torres Strait Islands.

In 1971, Neville Bonner became the first Aboriginal person to serve in Australia's government. He fought for the rights of his people.

COMING TO AUSTRALIA

Because it was so long ago, no one is exactly sure how the Indigenous peoples got to Australia. Some people who study history believe they made boats and crossed the ocean from Asia. Others believe the water level was so low back then that they simply walked over.

GOVERNMENT

Because Australia is part of the British Commonwealth, the leader of the country is the king or queen of England. However, a leader called the prime minister is in charge of running Australia's government.

FACT!
Australian law says that everyone over the age of 18 must vote.

Canberra (shown here) is Australia's capital city. Each state also has its own capital.

Australia's government has three parts, or branches. The legislative branch makes the laws. In Australia, this branch is called Parliament. It has two parts: the Senate and the House of Representatives. The Senate has 76 members. The House of Representatives has 150 members.

The judicial branch, which includes the courts, makes sure the laws are fair. The prime minister, deputy (assistant) prime minister, **governor-general**, and **cabinet** make up the executive branch. They make sure people follow the laws.

NO TERM LIMITS

Many countries have a term limit for their leader. This is the longest amount of time the leader can keep their position. For example, in the United States, a president can serve only two four-year terms, even if people want to vote for them a third time. Australia has no term limit for its prime minister.

In 2022, voters elected Anthony Albanese as the 31st prime minister of Australia.

THE ECONOMY

As of 2023, Australia has the 13th-largest **economy** in the world. Most of its workers have service jobs. This means that instead of making things, they do things such as teaching, working in hotels, and running stores.

Australia's main exports, or things that are sold to other countries, are coal, iron, natural gas, and gold. Its main imports, or things it buys from other countries, are oil, cars, and cell phones.

The picture on the left shows what gold mines used to look like in the 1800s. Today, modern machines are used to dig open-pit mines (below).

In the countryside, farmers grow many crops. One of the biggest crops grown in Australia is wheat. Farmers also grow many kinds of fruits, including bananas, mangoes, and pineapples.

RAISING CATTLE

Raising cattle for meat is a big part of the Australian economy. This can be a problem for the **environment**. When cows burp, they release a gas called methane. This can trap heat in the air and make the planet warmer, which leads to **climate change**.

FACT!

Australia's main trading partners are China, Japan, South Korea, India, and Hong Kong.

Australia has many vineyards, or places where wine is made. Australian wine is sold around the world.

THE ENVIRONMENT

Many of the animals in Australia are dangerous. Great white sharks, bull sharks, and blue-ringed octopuses swim in the waters. **Venomous** snakes and spiders live on land. Even kangaroos can be dangerous. One kick can kill a full-grown person.

However, Australia also has some of the most beautiful and unique, or one-of-a-kind, natural places. The Great Barrier Reef, off the coast of the state of Queensland, is the world's largest coral reef system. Sadly, the corals are dying because of climate change and other human actions.

The TV show Bluey is about a family of blue heelers. This is a species, or kind, of dog from Australia.

Australia is very dry, and climate change is making it even drier. The country often suffers from **droughts** that kill crops. Droughts can also cause huge wildfires. The worst wildfires in the country's history happened in late 2019 and early 2020. Nearly 3 billion animals died or lost their homes.

FACT!

About 80 percent of the plants and animals in Australia can't be found in the wild anywhere else in the world. They include koalas, eucalyptus trees, and wombats.

The Australian box jellyfish is the most venomous marine, or ocean, animal in the world. Its sting can badly hurt or even kill a person.

A FAKE ANIMAL

There are many real dangerous animals in Australia—and one fake one! Australians like to play a trick to scare visitors by telling them to watch out for drop bears. This made-up animal is said to drop on people from the trees.

THE PEOPLE TODAY

Australia is a very diverse country. This means that the 26 million people who live there come from a lot of different places and backgrounds. About 30 percent of the people living in Australia today were born in other countries. They have brought their own foods, languages, and practices to Australia.

FACT!

About 250 different Aboriginal languages are spoken in Australia today.

Sydney is the most populated city in Australia as well as in all of Oceania.

Although Indigenous peoples were the first ones in Australia, they make up only about 3 percent of the population today. This is because of racist actions taken against them when the Europeans first came to the country. Today, even though the Australian population is very diverse, nearly 100 percent of the government is made up of white people.

PROBLEMS WITH SEXISM

In 2022, several studies found that Australia has a big problem with sexism. This means that many men look down on women and treat them poorly. For example, Australian women are paid much less for the same work men do.

This picture shows two Aboriginal girls smiling for the camera.

LIFESTYLE

Most Australians live in cities on the country's coast. This makes the cities very crowded, so many people live in apartments. Australians in the city might drive places, or they might ride the bus or take the train. Many families in the cities have cell phones and computers. Life in the outback is slower than life in the cities. It's also more isolated, or lonely, in many places. However, there are some towns in the outback.

The outback town of Coober Pedy has homes, hotels, and restaurants underground. This helps people stay cool!

Farmers in the countryside grow all kinds of crops. Ranchers raise cattle and sheep. Some Australians work as miners. Others have jobs at wildlife parks or other places visitors come to see.

FACT!

Because of racism, it's hard for Indigenous people to get jobs, so many of them are poorer than white Australians.

Many people who live in the outback raise animals such as cows and sheep.

JOBS IN THE CITIES

People in Australian cities work in places such as law offices, banks, hospitals, and restaurants. About 62 percent of women and 70 percent of men have jobs outside the home.

RELIGION

Australia's government doesn't make rules based on any religion, or faith. It allows everyone to follow whatever religion they want—or no religion at all. About 44 percent of Australians are Christian. Australian Christians, like others around the globe, celebrate Christian holidays such as Christmas and Easter.

Because Australia is in the Southern Hemisphere, or half of the world, the seasons are swapped. They celebrate Christmas in December, but it's summer for them.

Other religions in Australia include Islam (3.2 percent), Hinduism (2.7 percent), and Buddhism (2.4 percent). The fastest-growing religion in Australia in recent decades is Hinduism. This religion has its roots in South Asia and is popular in India. Indigenous peoples have their own religions that they have followed for thousands of years.

FACT!

In Aboriginal religions, the period of time when the world was created by spirits is called the Dreamtime.

This picture shows one artist's idea of Julunggul. This is one name for an Aboriginal rainbow snake spirit who controls water and the weather.

CHANGING BELIEFS

All around the world, people have been getting less religious over time. In Australia, the amount of people who say they don't follow a religion has gone up from 6.7 percent in 1971 to 38.9 percent in 2021.

LANGUAGE

English is the most commonly spoken language in Australia. It's also the language most used by the country's government, schools, and businesses. However, Australian English has some different words than American or British English. These include "barbie" for barbecue, "drongo" for a silly person, and "sheila" for a girl.

FACT!

Many Aboriginal languages were lost because the Australian government made it illegal to speak them until the 1970s.

Aboriginal names for animals, such as koala, kangaroo, and wombat (shown here), have become part of the English language.

Many Australians speak languages other than English. More than 1 percent of the country's population speaks each of the following languages: Chinese (both Mandarin and Cantonese), Italian, Arabic, Greek, and Vietnamese.

Australian kids often learn other languages at school, including Japanese, French, and some Aboriginal languages. In some parts of Australia, classes are taught in Aboriginal languages and the students learn English as their second language.

This sign in New South Wales is written in both Bunjulung (an Aboriginal language, also spelled Bundjalung) and English.

UNOFFICIAL LANGUAGES

An official language is one a country decides will be the language the government uses. Many countries have more than one. Although the Australian government mainly uses English, Australia is one of only five countries in the world without an official language.

ARTS AND FESTIVALS

Art is a big part of the Australian way of life, or culture. Aboriginal artists have their own style of painting, which is often called dot art. Clifford Possum Tjapaltjarri is one well-known Aboriginal artist. In some parts of Australia, there are Aboriginal cave drawings that are thousands of years old.

FACT!

Chris Hemsworth, who plays Thor, and Margot Robbie, who plays Barbie, are two famous Australian actors.

This picture shows dot art on a boomerang.

Music is also an important part of Australian culture. Popular bands from Australia include AC/DC, INXS, and a children's band called The Wiggles. The didgeridoo is a wooden Aboriginal wind instrument. It makes a sound that's easy to recognize.

One important Australian holiday is Anzac Day on April 25. On this day, Australians remember people who have fought and died in past wars.

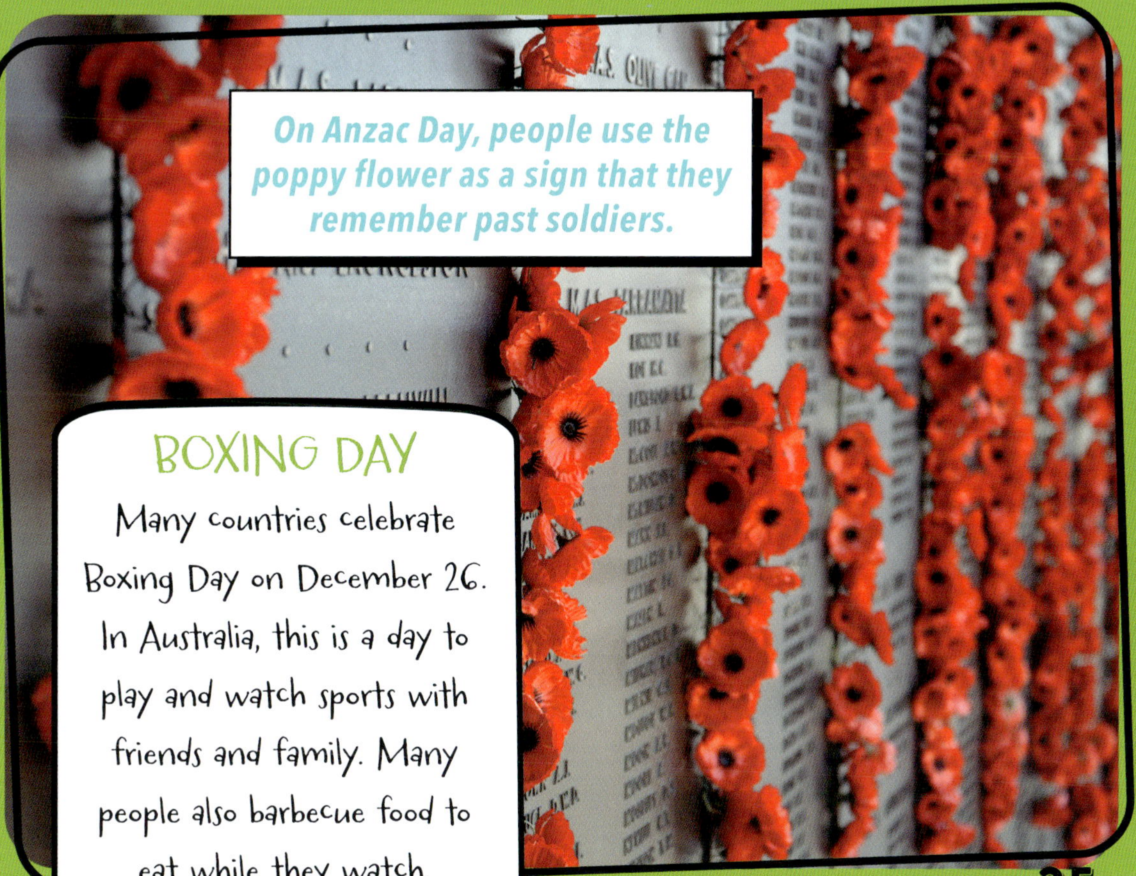

On Anzac Day, people use the poppy flower as a sign that they remember past soldiers.

BOXING DAY

Many countries celebrate Boxing Day on December 26. In Australia, this is a day to play and watch sports with friends and family. Many people also barbecue food to eat while they watch.

FUN AND PLAY

Watching and playing sports are two very popular activities in Australia. One of the most popular sports is Australian Rules Football. This sport, which is often called "Aussie rules" or "footy," is a bit like rugby. Cricket is also popular in Australia. The British brought it to the country.

FACT!
People from around the world come to Australia to swim near the Great Barrier Reef.

When thrown correctly, a boomerang will return to its owner.

Australians also love to spend time near the water. Swimming and surfing are popular with families as well as sports stars.

Popular outdoor games in Australia include lawn bowling, jump rope, and handball. Card games and board games are played by people of all ages. Australians also enjoy going out to eat or having a barbecue at home as a way to spend time with loved ones.

A WORLDWIDE TOY

For thousands of years, Aboriginal peoples used wood or bone boomerangs to hunt animals at a distance. Today, the boomerang has become a toy that is popular all over the world. However, it's still an important part of Aboriginal culture.

On nice days, Australian beaches such as Sydney's Bondi Beach (shown here) can get very crowded.

FOOD

Meat is a big part of many meals in Australia. This includes beef, chicken, and lamb as well as seafood such as shrimp, salmon, shark, and oysters. Meat pie is also a favorite.

People in Australia enjoy eating many different fruits. Passion fruit and papaya are two fruits that grow well in Australia. Adults often drink tea, coffee, and wine or beer. Many kids enjoy sweet drinks.

Vegemite is one of Australia's most famous foods. It's a salty, dark brown paste that's usually eaten on bread.

Foods that are indigenous to Australia are called bush tucker. These foods are what Aboriginal peoples have lived on in the outback for many years. Some examples include kangaroo meat, wild orange, and a kind of bug called the witchetty grub.

PAVLOVA

Pavlova is a dessert made from whipped egg whites, called meringue, and topped with fruit and whipped cream. It was named in honor of Anna Pavlova, a Russian ballerina who visited Australia and New Zealand in 1926. Australians and New Zealanders each say their country invented it!

FACT!
Shark meat is known as "flake" in Australia.

Bush tucker can be cooked in a pot over a campfire.

GLOSSARY

cabinet: People who help the leader of a government.

climate change: A change in the Earth's weather over a long period of time that is caused by human activities.

Commonwealth: An independent country that was once part of the British Empire and has kept some ties to Britain.

continent: One of the seven major masses of land on Earth.

democracy: A system of government where citizens choose their leaders.

drought: A period of time during which there is very little or no rain.

economy: The way goods and services are made and sold.

environment: The natural world around us.

governor-general: A person who takes the place of the English king or queen in important meetings in Australia.

racism: The practice of treating others poorly because they are part of a different race or ethnic group.

territory: A piece of land that is owned and controlled by another country but is not fully part of that country.

valuable: Having great worth or importance.

variety: The state of having many different things.

venomous: Able to produce a liquid poison that is forced into prey through fangs or stingers.

FIND OUT MORE

Books

Edwards, Sue Bradford. *Australia*. Minneapolis, MN: Essential Library, 2023.

Sabelko, Rebecca. *Australia*. Minneapolis, MN: Bellwether Media, 2023.

Vallepur, Shalini. *Australia*. New York, NY: Enslow Publishing, 2022.

Websites

Kids World Travel Guide: Australia
www.kids-world-travel-guide.com/australia-facts.html
Read more about Australia, take a look at some cool pictures of the country, and take a quiz to test your knowledge.

***National Geographic Kids*: Australia**
kids.nationalgeographic.com/geography/countries/article/australia
Learn more cool facts about Australia.

Video

Socratica Kids: Australian Animals
https://www.youtube.com/watch?v=TkCq54_ho-A
Learn about some of Australia's unique—and sometimes dangerous—animals.

Publisher's note to educators and parents: Our editors have carefully reviewed these websites to ensure that they are suitable for students. Many websites change frequently, however, and we cannot guarantee that a site's future contents will continue to meet our high standards of quality and educational value. Be advised that students should be closely supervised whenever they access the internet.

INDEX